X

HOW TO GET YOUR BUSINESS FOUND

X

HOW TO GET YOUR BUSINESS FOUND

The Business Owner Manual Series

SEBASTIAN ALONGI

SIGILLUM PUBLISHERS
TRACY, CA.

First Edition, May 2018.

ISBN 978-1-938898-08-2

Copyright © 2018 by Sigillum Publishers.

Published by Sigillum Publishers
896 Lourence Dr., Tracy. CA 95376
SigillumPublishers.com

Cover and interior design by A.C. Alongi
AnaAlongi.com

Printed in the United States of America.

TABLE OF CONTENTS

I was inspired to write this booklet when I was working for a merchant services provider in corporate America. At the time, I was astonished by the number of businesses that close their doors every day and I decided that those statistics, or sad reality, was unacceptable.

I always had a deep respect for entrepreneurs and business owners, because I grew up in a family where my father, despite not being highly educated, was able to start multiple ventures and provide for our family.

I'm not going to lie to you. It wasn't easy for my father either; at times he did well and at times he had epic failures. You see, as are all entrepreneurs and business owners, he was great at what he knew, (his area of expertise), but running a business today requires the ability to establish workable systems. To do so, you either need to find the right people that bring to the table a different skillset, or you need to implement the tools that accomplish distinct functions while you still do what you do best.

You see, smart business owners surround themselves with other smart professionals that are good at what they do. By doing so, they form a team of experts, each bringing to the table a unique perspective.

It is impossible for a business owner to know everything. With that said, a business owner should know how to recognize good opportunities and systems to ensure that all vital functions of running a business are performed efficiently.

The Business Owner Manual booklet series are written to give business owners know-how about specific topics in a quick and concise manner.

INTRODUCTION

In my quest for helping businesses, I've learned that no matter what you know, or what your product does, in order for a business to survive, it needs new customers coming in through your door or website consistently, and in a cost-effective way.

Customers are the fuel that keep your business running! If you don't have new customers coming in, then soon you will run out of fuel (cash-flow) and a whole new series of problems begin.

Getting new customers require two things:

Letting people (your potential customers) know that your business exists.

Being visible enough for your potential customers to find you.

To let people know that your business exists, you must find communications lines and channels to reach customers and potential customers. These are the places where your potential customers go when they seek information about products and services.

Finding the channels is a first step, because once you do, guess what? You're going to find other businesses just like yours fighting for top placement within each channel, so it is important to learn what you can do better to differentiate yourself and stand out against your competitors.

The secret is to learn how to stand out and to be better at providing the answers that your potential customers are seeking.

In today's society, people get bombarded with ads, messages, posts, videos, news—the options are infinite. If a business is to survive, it must become proficient at the game of cutting through the noise to capture its customer's attention.

Have you ever tried to talk to someone who was obviously distracted thinking about something else? What kind of result did you get from such conversation?

You are fighting for attention!

Without getting your prospect's attention, you're not even in the game.

Even if you grab their attention partially, how long can you keep their attention on you? How do you keep your business in the forefront of their mind so that when they are ready to purchase, they think of you first?

These are all things that you need to consider when thinking about your online digital presence, as well as other customer acquisition strategies.

My goal with this booklet is to help you understand what you can do to boost your business visibility.

Sebastian Alongi | Author

CHAPTER ONE

YOUR PROBLEM
IS INVISIBILITY

CHAPTER ONE

YOUR PROBLEM IS INVISIBILITY

Before a person can purchase products or services from you, they need to know that you exist. You might assume that putting your business on Google, or Facebook, is enough for people to find you, but in reality, it takes a lot more to boost your visibility.

It used to be that when we needed information about a business, we looked in the Yellow Pages to find the type of business we were looking for. Back then, the options were more limited and we had to believe what the publisher was advertising, but things have changed.

With the internet, we're now able to learn the good, the bad, and the ugly about any business in seconds. Also, before making a buying decision, we look for information from peers and other consumers and read about their experiences, and if this information is negative? Oh boy… your bottom line suffers like there is no tomorrow.

The reality is that we carry in our hands more computer power than was ever possible in prior decades, and things keep evolving in giant leaps. Maybe a few years ago, people were using their desktop computers to find your business, but now people search for businesses in on their mobile phones, voice commands, GPS, and more. The next big trend is Artificial Intelligence (AI) and it is happening now. You see and hear people searching for answers using Siri from Apple, Alexa from Amazon, *"Hey google"* from Google, and so on.

Not long ago, I went to a conference where the CEO of a Knowledge Management Platform gave a demonstration and asked Alexa, *"Where can I eat a broccoli cheddar soup,"* and Alexa came back with the closest Panera location, as their menu was available on the internet. Local search is moving in this direction and it is not going to be long before it becomes the primary way we find answers.

When a person, your prospect, asks a question that is relevant to the products and services that you offer, it is essential to know what information to provide on the search engines and internet directories, so that they showcase your business as the best possible answer to the prospect's search query.

When you don't take the necessary actions to provide good, accurate and consistent data to the search engines and search platforms, these will rank your business as less relevant and push you down the hierarchy of responses.

We live in a society where we want things fast. No one wants to browse through pages and pages of results. If your info doesn't come up on the top of the search engines result pages, then you have a huge problem with visibility that needs to get fixed right away.

The bad news is that invisibility is costing you money. The good news is that it can be easily fixed when you implement the right tools to boost and enhance your business visibility.

CHAPTER TWO

ARE YOU IN CONTROL OF THE INFORMATION THAT EXIST ABOUT YOUR BUSINESS?

ARE YOU IN CONTROL OF THE INFORMATION THAT EXIST ABOUT YOUR BUSINESS?

The internet hosts hundreds of publishers and directories that only exist to provide users with information about businesses.

While the number of users that each directory or publisher has varies, most of them are prominent enough that it is important to ensure that proper information about your business resides within their platform.

Some of the best directories will call you to sell you advertisement or enhanced placement, but more often than not, you don't get called by each directory to ask you about your business.

Surprising enough, your business information exists in more directories that you would suspect. If they didn't call you, however, it means that they got their information about your business from an external source. What happens if that other source had a different business name (a variation), or a wrong address, or an old phone number?

What happens is that you lose clients that are searching for your business type. If they call and the number is wrong, they won't keep searching for your business; instead, they'll move to the next available record and so on.

Missing, inaccurate, or incorrect information propagates over the Internet like a virus, because other publishers and directories will pull the contact data as correct and make it public despite being incorrect.

Large search engines like Google, Bing, and Yahoo, scrape all over the Internet to rank information. Their goal is to provide the user the best possible answer to their search queries.

Most directories publish what is called NAP Data. NAP stands for Name, Address, and Phone Number.

Each site that has information about your business is considered a citation.

In cataloging businesses to rank them by relevancy, the search engines send bots, (software to gather information that exists on the internet), and if the information about your business is not consistent on all sites, then your ranking is affected.

Imagine that you were asking ten different people about a pizza place in Livermore, CA and each person gave you a different name, or a different address. How reliable would that information be to you?

What would happen if you asked the same question to ten different people that really knew the place, and each gave you the same answer. Would you trust their information?

The procedure the search engine uses is similar, except that as a human you can recognize a small variation in a name and realize it is the same place. That's not always the case with software.

As a business owner that cares for his business and its brand, you need to make sure that all the information that exists on the Internet is *accurate* and *under your control.*

You're probably thinking, "I get it, that's great; how do I do that?"

CHAPTER THREE

KNOWLEDGE IS POWER

CHAPTER THREE

KNOWLEDGE IS POWER

I remember watching one of the Spider Man movies starring Tobey Maguire and hearing Uncle Ben telling Peter (Spider Man) something like, *"With power comes responsibility"*.

Knowledge gives you power. Power to defend yourself, power of choice, power to act, and power to prevent unwanted outcomes.

For knowledge to be useful, it needs to be accompanied by control and responsibility.

In this case, we're talking about having control of the information that exists about your business on the internet. Responsibility means taking full ownership and being accountable for the outcomes resulting from your actions or inactions.

You can read this booklet as an outsider, not really engaging with its content, or you can absorb the information with the purpose of finding key concepts to grow your business.

If you intend to take ownership, then it is important to realize that it is up to you to tell the story about your business, because nothing good can come from leaving it to chance.

You have probably heard the phrase, *"What you don't know can't hurt you"*.

I find this phrase to be untrue.

You may not know that your business information online

is inaccurate, and it would hurt your business.

You may not know that you have negative reviews on some platform and it is definitively impacting your business.

Ignorance is not a blessing, nor an excuse, so naturally the first step toward handling your digital presence is to find out all the places that provide information about your business and whether that information is accurate.

Lucky for you, many business listing management providers offer a free **business scan** tool that allows you to enter the information about your business and a few seconds or minutes later, depending on the provider, the scan will tell you how your information appears online.

Once you know how your information appears online, it is a matter of deciding what's the best way to fix the information.

You need to find a way that is effective, affordable, and that really solves this problem for you.

At this point, some of you are thinking of going to each directory and fixing the information yourself. The problem with that is:

- You would need to keep a user name and password for each directory.
- There is no guarantee that they will take and fix your information.
- Even if they did, there is no telling how long the directory would take to fix it.
- Many directories will charge you, so going individually to each directory isn't cost effective.
- If you have ever changed any information, you would have to go back to each directory and change the information again.

While I can come up with more bullet points illustrating why going direct is not practical, I feel I have made my point.

Before talking about potential solutions, let's bring home the importance of search engines, directories and publishers by looking at some of the top business listings platforms and its numbers.

Major Search Engines by Number of Visitors

Google	175,177,915
Yahoo	98,108,167
Bing	76,109,601

Social Media Networks by Number of Visitors

Facebook	115,493,383
Twitter	74,664,547
LinkedIn	57,941,255
Instagram	43,631,715

Other Directories and Publishers by Number of Visitors

These are some of the hundreds of directories that exist online

Yelp	36,391,143
WhitePages	17,567,949
MapQuest	15,671,430
Foresquare	4,542,593
SuperPages	2,764,093
411	2,116,546
MerchantCircle	1,055,134
YP	818,923
Chamber of Commerce	625,012
City Search	610,530
HotFrog	340,131

Kudzu	244,098
ShowMeLocal	111,713
EZLocal	104,546
eLocal	69,752
8Coupons	66,178

All these platforms heavily promote their platform and they have the users that your website doesn't have. Also, many of these platforms have longevity and are considered a trusted source of information by the search engines, and therefore they are ranked higher than most websites. In fact, most of the time when you search for something, the first few top results are one of these platforms.

There is nothing wrong with it if you can leverage their power in your favor.

Your potential customers visit these directories when they are searching for information. Some of these directories are niche or industry specific, but many of them are generic and applicable to all industries.

When acquiring a Business Listing Management solution, one of the things to look for is what is the number of directories their platform connects with, and whether the platform offers directories that are specific to your industry.

Not all Business Listing Solutions are made the same. Some of the things to look for are:

1. **Number of directories and their relevance.** Some might offer more directories but omit major ones.
2. **Type of connectivity.** How does the Business Listing Management Platform connect with the directories, and how long does it take for your information to go live?

3. **Content Allowed.** What other information fields are you allowed to provide? Some platforms enable you to enter NAP data, plus a few additional fields, while other platforms permit you to add a lot more information such as: menus, business hours, holiday hours, videos, staff bios, etc. Studies show that platforms that allow more enhanced information generate more visitor actions.

4. **Control of your business information.** Does the provider have some sort of lock that prevents incorrect data to filter into the directories?

5. **Updates & Changes.** How long does it take to push changes and updates?

6. **Call to Action.** Can you push coupons or special offers?

7. **Cancellation Consequences.** What happens if you cancel the service? Does your information revert to its original condition?

Most companies that provide these services combine it with other products and services, so the pricing for these types of services are widely ranged. Some companies give you the access, but you are expected to enter the information and maintain it to keep it current, while other companies would do most of the work for you. If you're not tech savvy, or don't have the time to update the platform, it is important to choose a provider that will do the work for you. Otherwise, you'll end up paying for a service that you don't fully use, or that gives you partial benefits instead of maximizing your hard-earned dollars.

SOLUTION TYPES AND ITS COMPARISON

CHAPTER FOUR

SOLUTION TYPES AND

ITS COMPARISON

By now, I hope that I have properly conveyed to you the importance of enhancing your online presence, enough for you to act. I could go on and elaborate or get more technical, but the purpose of this booklet is to provide key information simply, and free of gibberish.

In an ideal world, before making a purchase decision, you take your time to research and compare solutions, pricing, and so on. More often, you are presented with a solution to a problem and then you decide on the spot. Therefore, you should at least have a vague idea of the type of solutions that exist.

X

DIGITAL KNOWLEDGE
MANAGEMENT SOLUTIONS

— Comparison Chart —

Solution Attribute	Manual	Data Aggregator	API Submission	Yext
Approach	Manual	Automated	Automated	Automated
Network	1 at a time	Variable	Variable	80+ and aggregators
Real-Time Updates	N/A	No	Variable	Majority
Suppresses Duplicates	No	No	No	Majority
Locks Data	No	No	No	Majority
Google My Business API	Yes	No	Variable	Yes
Apple Maps	Yes	Variable	No	Yes
InfoGroup	N/A	Yes	Variable	Yes
Neustar/ Localeze	N/A	Yes	Variable	Yes
Acxiom	N/A	Yes	Variable	Yes
Enhanced Content	Variable	No	Variable	Majority

KEY ATTRIBUTES BY BULLET POINT

There are many solutions available on how a business can manage their digital knowledge online. This guide will help you understand the main attributes of each solution.

MANUAL SUBMISSION

- Free but requires tremendous manpower.
- Not all sites allow you to claim business listings, so you need to be accurate on all of them to be fully optimized for searches.
- Human error is likely and causes inaccuracy and inaccuracy erodes SEO and can cause duplicate listings, as well as customer confusion.
- To keep up with all the changes to your clients' data, from database refreshes, user-suggested edits, and other factors, you'll need to manually submit 24/7.
- Does not provide definitive control, because data can be overwritten at any time.

DATA AGGREGATOR

- Relatively inexpensive— you pay for your data to be included in datasets, which they then sell to various buyers, including local listing sites, search engines, and more.
- "Hope and pray" solution— your clients' information must be purchased by a publisher to have a chance of getting published.
- When clients' data is purchased, it goes through a March Madness-style tournament of data evaluation, because

publishers gather and consider data from a number of other sources, including government records, tax forms, user-generated content, stock filings, phone directories, social media posts, and more.

- Your business data may get published, but publishers are constantly refreshing their databases, as often as a few times a day.
- Data is always at risk of being overwritten with no real-time control and no functionality to support enhanced content like menus, photos, videos, and other important details.

API SUBMISSION

- May be cheaper than Match & Lock API solutions— may claim to be just as good.
- Simply a method of sending data to the publisher— data is being submitted, but not correctly matched or locked.
- Does not guarantee definitive or real-time control— data is still at risk of being overwritten by user-suggested edits.

YEXT

- You are paying for the industry's best technology and most robust network of publishers.
- Manages and updates clients' business data across Google, Facebook, Yahoo, Bing, Yelp, Foursquare and about 70+ more publishers.
- Pioneer of Match & Lock™ technology, which automatically scans, locates, and claims your existing business listings on sites across the PowerListings Network

when you go live. Scans every publisher's database — rather than scraping its consumer-facing site — to find the listing you want to control. When a match is identified, it immediately locks that listing so no other data source can alter the information.

- On those sites that support Match & Lock, clients' business information is locked, and it cannot be overwritten, regardless of when the publisher refreshes their database, or whether or not users submit suggested edits.

CHAPTER FIVE

LOST INCOME

CHAPTER FIVE

LOST INCOME

Lost income can be defined as the amount of revenue that you should be making based on your existing resources, but that for one reason or another, you are not making.

Let's say you have a hair salon with four hairdressers. Each hairdresser has the capability to service four people in an hour. Assuming that each hairdresser works eight hours with an average ticket size of $15.00, your potential revenue each day is $1,920.00.

Now, let's say that it is Tuesday and your hairdressers are only servicing two people each hour; your revenue for that day would be $960.00. This day your production was $960.00 short of your producing capacity, so that day you lost $960.00 in potential revenue.

If this happens twice a week, your lost income will look like this:

Weekly Lost Income: $1,920.00
Monthly Lost Income: $8,256.00
Yearly Lost Income: $99,072.00

Every time your potential customers can't find your business, it is costing you money.

This formula is applicable to all businesses. If you own a restaurant, then your formula would be based on your seating capacity and average ticket size.

The point is that as a business owner your role is to work toward reaching your maximum delivery capacity, even break it, and scale your business to a complete new level of revenue capacity.

When deciding if you should invest on a business listings management tool or not, keep in mind that invisibility equals poverty and will cost you more than anything you will pay for services that list your business on the Internet.

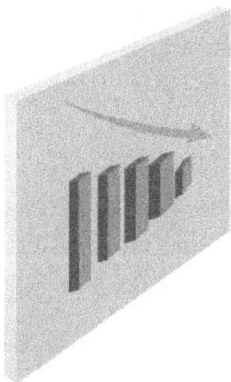

LIFETIME VALUE OF A CUSTOMER

CHAPTER SIX

LIFETIME VALUE OF A CUSTOMER

A nother factor to consider when acquiring a business tool or system is the LIFETIME VALUE OF A CUSTOMER- LTV for short.

What is the lifetime value of a customer in your business?

Before giving the formula to calculate the LTV, let me give you an example from my own experience.

When I was working in corporate America, about once a week, I used to eat at a Sushi Restaurant located near my company's headquarters. I had two or three different meals that I usually ordered, but to round up the numbers, each time I ate at the Sushi Restaurant I spent around $15.00. If you multiply $15.00 for 52 weeks in a year, then that restaurant was making just on me around $780.00 yearly—me, just one customer. I followed that routine for at least five years, so my LTV for the Sushi Restaurant was approximately $3,900.00.

I don't remember how I found that particular Sushi place. I probably Googled "Sushi Near Me" or something like that. The point is that whatever they used to attract me, it brought the restaurant $3,900.00 that they were previously not making, and I doubt that they spent that much to acquire me.

The example above is the math for one client, but what if having an enhanced digital presence opens the door for your business to acquire two, three, four, or five customers per day, week, or even a month? How much additional revenue is that for your business?

At this point, if someone was presenting me this information, I would probably say, "Fine how do I know that getting my business listed will get me comparable results?"

My answer is straightforward: You have to risk it to get the biscuit!

In other words, if you don't do anything, or don't change anything, then the outcome will be nothing, zero, zilch, nada!

Being a business owner or manager is about taking measured risks and trying things, despite sometimes being uncomfortable due to the unknowns connected with making a decision. Then again, you already decided to play the game when you opened your doors, so now that you're in the game, it's best to play to win because of this simple rule:

"Nothing stays the same in this world, things either expand or contract!"

This doesn't mean that you should blindly purchase all the products and services that are offered to you. Business smarts involves measuring ROI, monitoring results, and knowing when to cut things that don't result in a positive ROI.

When selecting a business listing management platform, it is important to ask the provider what analytics are available through their platform. The type of Key Performance Indications (KPIs) recorded by these platforms are profile views, clicks, live directories, calls, Yelp actions, and so on.

If the platform offered to you doesn't offer analytics, I would recommend staying away from it.

THERE IS NO BETTER TIME THAN RIGHT NOW

CHAPTER SEVEN

THERE IS NO BETTER TIME THAN RIGHT NOW

The best time to take action is the present.

When we leave things for later, procrastinate, and add things to a future "To Do" list, what usually happens is no action. Then you forget all about it, and in the meantime, every day that goes by becomes another day where customers are not finding you.

My company does offer these services, but I didn't write this booklet to sell you my services, I wrote it to help you understand the importance of your digital presence and how it does affect your business, so here is a list of places where you can find business listing management solutions.

Remember, the first thing you want to do is to run a "business scan" and find out how your business appears online.

List of Providers:
Prodigio: www.clientsformula.com/yext
Yext: www.yext.com
Vendasta: www.vendasta.com
Manta: www.manta.com
GoDaddy: https://www.godaddy.com/online-marketing/local-business-listings

Yahoo: https://www.yext.com/pl/yahoo-claims/index.html
ShowMeLocal: www.showmelocal.com

I hope you find this booklet useful and I would love to hear your feedback and success stories implementing these solutions.
To ask a question about Business Management Solutions, email me at sebastian@prodigiousa.com .

Best of luck! Sebastian Alongi

Prodigio
Client Enhancement & Acquisition Strategies

Sebastian Alongi
Co-founder & CEO

Phone 866.427.4891
Sebastian@prodigiousa.com
www.clientsformula.com

To take action and fix your online digital presence got to:

www.clientsformula.com/yext

Use coupon code:

SAVE20